ANCIENT CIVILIZATIONS

The Aztecs

DISCARDED

by Anita Ganeri

Compass Point Books ✦ Minneapolis, Minnesota

First American edition published in 2007 by
Compass Point Books
3109 West 50th St., #115
Minneapolis, MN 55410

THE AZTECS
was produced by
David West Children's Books
7 Princeton Court
55 Felsham Road
London SW15 1AZ

 This book was manufactured with paper containing
at least 10 percent post-consumer waste.

Illustrator: Carl Lyons
Designer: David West
Editors: Kate Newport, Robert McConnell
Page Production: Bobbie Nuytten
Content Adviser: Robert J. Sharer,
  Shoemaker Professor in Anthropology,
  University of Pennsylvania Museum

Library of Congress Cataloging-in-Publication Data
Ganeri, Anita, 1961-
   The Aztecs / by Anita Ganeri—1st American ed.
      p. cm.—(Ancient civilizations)
   Includes bibliographical references and index.
   ISBN: 978-0-7565-1950-6 (hardcover)
   ISBN: 978-0-7565-1952-0 (paperback)
   1. Aztecs—History—Juvenile literature. 2. Aztecs—
Social life and customs—Juvenile literature.   I. Title.
II. Series: Ancient civilizations (Minneapolis, Minn.)
F1219.73.G35 2006
972'.01—dc22   2006002991

Visit Compass Point Books on the Internet at *www.compasspointbooks.com*
or e-mail your request to *custserv@compasspointbooks.com*

Contents

DISCARDED

The Aztecs

The great Aztec empire ruled in Mexico about 500 years ago. The Aztecs were fierce warriors, but they also had one of the most advanced civilizations in the world. They built great cities and temples to their gods, and they created great works of art. Although the Aztecs lived many years ago, we know a lot about them.

Look out for this man digging up interesting items from the past, like this animal-shaped pot.

4

Who Were the Aztecs?

The Aztecs were the people who lived in Mexico from about 800 years ago until 400 years ago. They traveled to Mexico from the north because of a terrible drought in their homeland. According to legend, the Aztecs then wandered for many years until they settled in one place and built the great capital city of Tenochtitlan.

Every Aztec boy dreamed of becoming a great warrior. He was made a full warrior when he had taken three prisoners of war. The best warriors were richly rewarded for their bravery in battle.

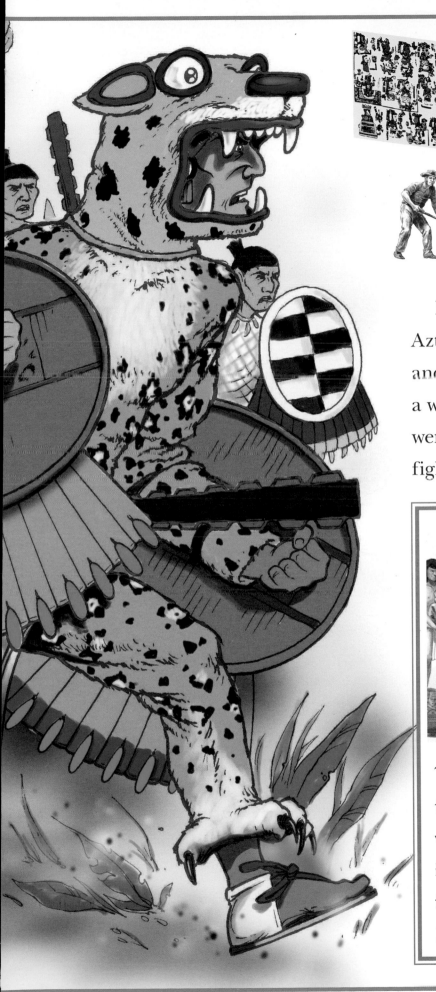

We have a lot of information about Aztec life, laws, customs, and religion from the few surviving Aztec books, called codices.

Based in Tenochtitlan, the mighty Aztec army conquered a huge empire and kept it under control. War was a way of life for the Aztecs, and boys were trained to handle weapons and fight from an early age.

The Aztecs collected tributes from the people they conquered. Those who did not pay were punished. Goods included gold, precious stones, and feathers. One tribute list even included 16,000 rubber balls.

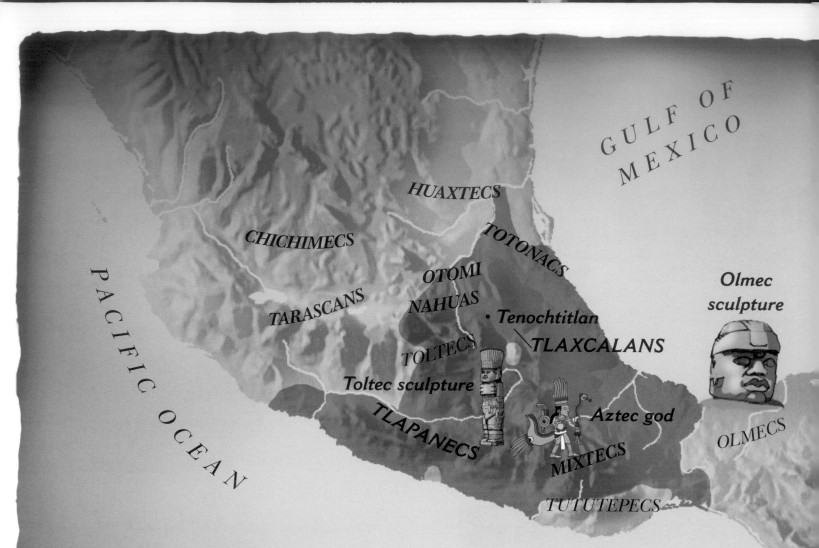

GULF OF MEXICO

HUAXTECS

CHICHIMECS

TOTONACS

OTOMI
NAHUAS

TARASCANS

• Tenochtitlan

Olmec sculpture

TLAXCALANS

TOLTECS

Toltec sculpture

Aztec god

TLAPANECS

PACIFIC OCEAN

OLMECS

MIXTECS

TUTUTEPECS

The Aztec World

The most important and most powerful person in Aztec society was the emperor. He was called *Huei Tlatoani*, or Great Speaker. He was chosen from the members of the royal family by a group of high-ranking nobles.

The emperor lived in a great palace in the center of Tenochtitlan, surrounded by officials, nobles, servants, and his many wives and children.

At the height of its power, the Aztec empire, shown in red, stretched from coast to coast across Mexico. Tribes lived in various areas of the empire.

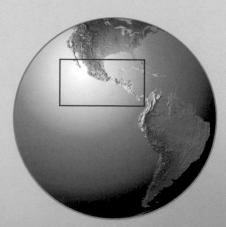

The Aztec World

Carvings show how the Aztecs copied aspects of Toltec life and culture.

YUCATAN
PENINSULA

Mayan temple

MAYANS

The emperor was head of the Aztec government and leader of the army. He ruled the country, decided when to go to war, received tributes from conquered lands, and held talks with neighboring people.

The emperor was so important that ordinary people were not allowed to look at him. Even nobles had to change their fine clothes for rough blankets and go barefoot in his presence. After their audience with him, they had to walk out backward.

Capital City

Tenochtitlan was founded on an island in Lake Texcoco about 750 years ago. It grew very quickly, both in size and power. At the height of the empire, 500 years ago, the city may have been home to more than 200,000 people.

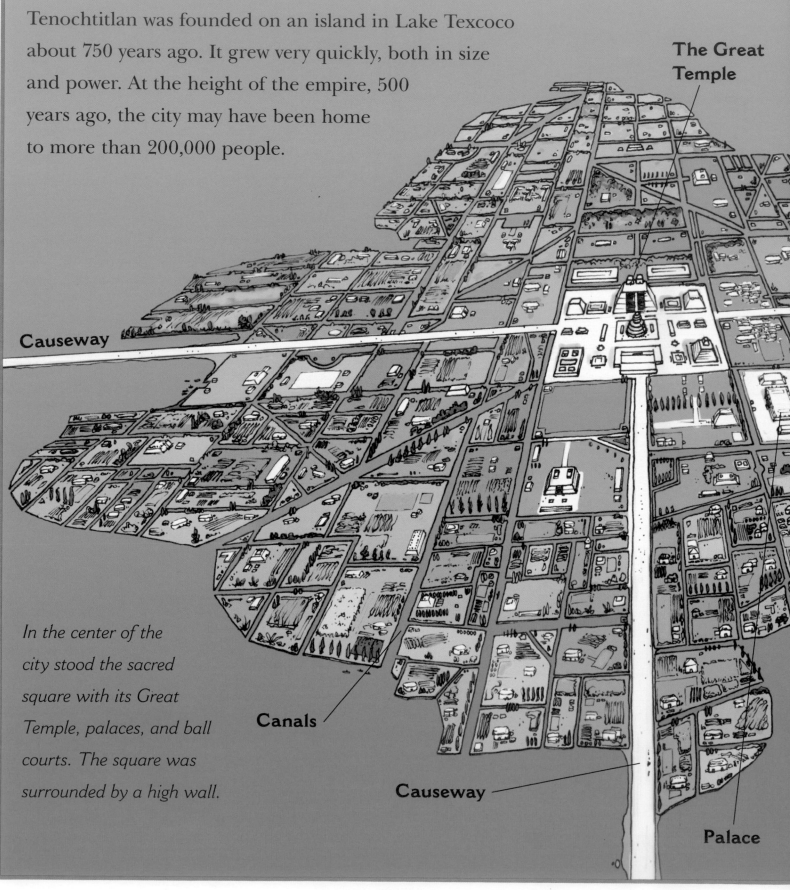

The Great Temple

In the center of the city stood the sacred square with its Great Temple, palaces, and ball courts. The square was surrounded by a high wall.

Canals

Causeway

Causeway

Palace

Instead of streets, the city was crisscrossed by canals, and most people traveled by canoe. Paddling was quicker and easier than getting around the city on foot.

Causeway

The city was laid out on a grid pattern and was divided into four quarters. The city was linked to the mainland by three giant causeways. Gaps in the causeways were usually filled with massive pieces of timber. These were rolled away in wartime to stop enemy soldiers from attacking the city.

A map of Tenochtitlan made by Spanish invaders shows the Great Temple in the center of the city.

11

The Story of Tenochtitlan

Legend tells how the Aztecs built the great city of Tenochtitlan. After leaving their homeland, the Aztecs wandered through deserts, forests, and mountains for many years, searching for a place to settle. Four priests led their procession, carrying a great statue of Huitzilopochtli, the god of war. The Aztecs believed that he protected and guided them on their long journey.

After many months, they came to the Valley of Mexico, where they fought in the army of a local king. But the Aztecs killed the king's daughter, and he banished them from his kingdom. Once again, the Aztecs were homeless. They then took shelter on a marshy island in the middle of a swampy lake.

On this island, they saw the sign that the gods had promised them—an eagle perched on a prickly pear cactus, holding a snake in its beak. "You must build your city here," said the statue of Huitzilopochtli. So the Aztecs built their great city on the island in the lake. They called it Tenochtitlan—the place of the prickly pear.

At first, Tenochtitlan was simply a huddle of reed huts with a central temple dedicated to Huitzilopochtli. But it soon grew into the great Aztec capital.

The Great Temple in Tenochtitlan was the most important temple in the Aztec world.

The image of Coyolxauhqui, goddess of the moon, is carved into a stone that lay at the bottom of the stairs leading up to the Great Temple. The stone caught the bodies of victims sacrificed to the gods.

Gods and Goddesses

Religion was at the center of Aztec life. The Aztecs worshipped hundreds of gods and goddesses, believing that they controlled everything.

It was pointless to try to go against the gods' wishes. Instead, special ceremonies were held and human sacrifices were made to keep them happy. It was considered a great honor to die in this way. The most magnificent buildings in an Aztec city were the towering temples built to honor the gods.

To show their sacred position in society, Aztec priests wore dark clothes, painted their skin black, and let their hair grow long.

The Aztecs used a calendar based on the sun. A huge carving called the Calendar Stone depicts the face of the Aztec sun god Tonatiuh, in the center.

15

Sacred Games

The Aztecs' favorite sport was *ulama*, or the sacred ball game. The movement of the ball was thought to symbolize the daily journey of the sun across the sky. The ball game was played on a special stone court built close to the temples. Two teams of players tried to score points by hitting a solid rubber ball through a stone ring. It was easier said than done. They could only use their hips, elbows, and knees—not their heads, hands, or feet. Players were often badly injured. Thousands of people flocked to watch the exciting spectacle and to place bets on the result.

The stone rings were placed at awkward angles high up on a wall. This made it extremely difficult to score a goal.

The game of *patolli* was played on a cross-shaped board, divided into 52 parts like the 52 years in the Aztec calendar cycle. Players used dried beans as dice and stones as counters. The moves of the counters symbolized the passing of the years.

Ulama players wore thick padding on their arms and legs to protect themselves from the hard ball. Games were fiercely contested, as if they were real battles. No one wanted to lose. The defeated captain was sometimes sacrificed at the end of the game.

Family Life

Everyone in an Aztec family was expected to work hard. Children had to help their parents from an early age. Some boys went to the local school or a school attached to a temple. Most girls stayed at home and helped their mothers.

Children who misbehaved were forced to breathe smoke from burning hot chilies. This hurt their eyes and throats—a very harsh punishment.

A painting shows how important keeping clean was to the Aztecs. Most houses had a bathhouse like a modern sauna. This is where the family took regular steam baths.

Ordinary Aztec people lived in simple houses made from reeds or branches and plastered with clay. They had very little furniture in their houses. They sat on low stools or mats and slept on mats spread out on the floor.

The most important part of the house was the hearth where the family cooked their food. Wealthier families had larger houses made from mudbricks or stone, and they were built around a central courtyard.

The father was the head of an Aztec family. His job was to support the family, usually by doing craftwork or farming. His wife's duties included cooking, keeping the house, and weaving clothes.

Farming and Food

Aztec farmers just outside Tenochtitlan grew crops such as maize, fruit, vegetables, and flowers on plots of land called *chinampas*. These were like small islands in the lake. First, the farmer built a framework of twigs and branches. Then he covered it with rich, black mud from the bottom of the lake.

Maize harvested in September

Maize storage

Some chinampas had houses built on them.

Some favorite foods:

Kidney beans

Sweet potatoes

Mushrooms

Avocado

Tomato

Maize

Chilies

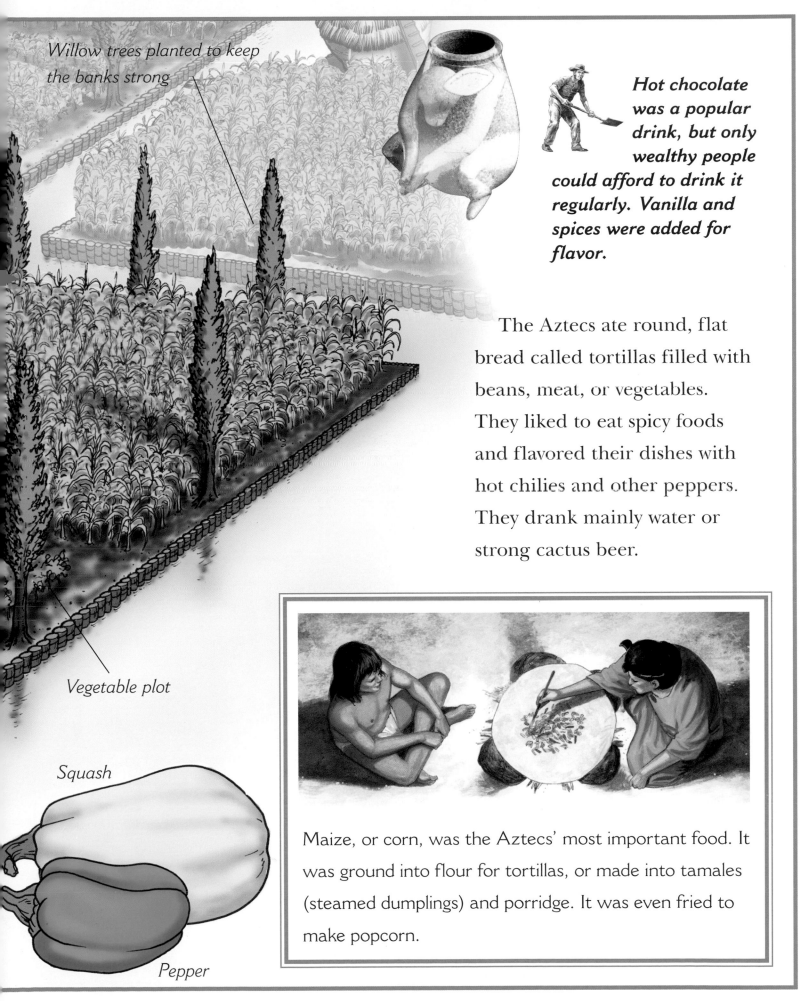

Willow trees planted to keep the banks strong

Hot chocolate was a popular drink, but only wealthy people could afford to drink it regularly. Vanilla and spices were added for flavor.

The Aztecs ate round, flat bread called tortillas filled with beans, meat, or vegetables. They liked to eat spicy foods and flavored their dishes with hot chilies and other peppers. They drank mainly water or strong cactus beer.

Vegetable plot

Squash

Pepper

Maize, or corn, was the Aztecs' most important food. It was ground into flour for tortillas, or made into tamales (steamed dumplings) and porridge. It was even fried to make popcorn.

Merchants and Markets

Aztec merchants, called *pochteca*, traveled far and wide to trade for goods such as gold, feathers, jaguar skins, and precious stones. These journeys lasted for weeks and even months. The merchants also worked as spies for the emperor and brought back information about his rivals from all over the empire.

Merchants usually traveled by night, when it was safer. They did not have wheeled transport but used porters to carry heavy loads of goods on their backs. It was very hard work.

The great market in the city of Tlatelolco was the largest and best in the region.

Here you could buy everything from food and firewood to pots and precious stones.

To pay for goods, the Aztecs used cocoa beans and feather quills filled with gold dust.

Merchants' goods were bought and sold at busy, bustling markets. The Aztecs did not use money. Much of the buying and selling was done through bartering or with cocoa beans or quills.

Market inspectors checked the goods carefully and made sure that the merchants charged a fair price.

Clothes and Society

In Aztec society, there were very strict rules about the type of clothes a person could and could not wear.

Clothes showed a person's rank in society, and it was a serious crime to wear clothes belonging to a richer or more powerful group. Offenders were sometimes put to death.

Wealthy Aztecs could afford to wear very expensive jewelry, like a gold nose plug. Gold and precious stones were also made into earrings, necklaces, and bracelets.

Rich Aztecs wore clothes made from cotton, but poor people wove their clothes from the fibers of the maguey cactus. This plant was also used to make rope, paper, nets, sandals, bags, and blankets.

For everyday use, ordinary Aztec men wore a simple loincloth around the waist with a cloak knotted over one shoulder. Women wore a long, loose blouse over a long skirt. Wealthy people wore similar clothes but in richer colors and finer materials. The amount of decoration on their clothes was another sign of their wealth and position in society.

Hairstyles also gave information about a person's status. Men who were warriors wore their hair in topknots. Women who were married wore their hair up.

Arts and Crafts

The Aztecs loved beautiful objects, and skilled craft workers were greatly valued in their society. They made ornate jewelry, fine pottery, brilliant wood carvings, stone sculptures, and beautiful mosaics from precious stones. Workers belonged to groups called guilds.

The Aztecs used feathers from many kinds of birds, but the most prized were the bright green feathers of the quetzal bird. Thousands of these birds were kept in the city aviary.

Often the feather worker's whole family helped him to make a headdress. Sons of feather workers and other craft workers usually followed in their fathers' footsteps.

The most respected craft workers were the *amanteca*, or feather workers. They used tropical bird feathers to make brightly colored cloaks and headdresses for high-ranking Aztec nobles and warriors. The feathers were washed and sorted. Then they were pasted onto stiffened cloth and decorated with gold and precious stones.

A beautiful quetzal feather headdress is said to have once belonged to Moctezuma, the last great Aztec emperor.

27

What Happened to the Aztecs?

By the early 1500s, the Aztec empire had reached the height of its power. But in 1519, Spanish invaders landed on the east coast of Mexico. Led by Hernán Cortés, they marched on the capital looking for Aztec gold.

At first, the Aztecs thought Cortés and his men were gods or friends. But Cortés seized the city and took the Aztec emperor, Moctezuma, prisoner. Moctezuma was later killed, and in 1521, the Aztecs were forced to surrender to the Spanish.

The monk Bernardino de Sahagun arrived in Mexico a few years after the fall of the Aztecs. He asked local artists to paint pictures of what life in Mexico used to be like.

At first, Moctezuma greeted Cortés warmly because he believed him to be the god Quetzalcoatl. But the Spanish brutally destroyed the Aztec world.

The Spanish reduced Tenochtitlan to ruins. Today, Mexico City stands on top of the ancient city. But some ruins, such as those of the Great Temple, have been found by archaeologists.

Glossary

archaeologists—people who study the past from ancient objects, such as pots, tools, and carvings

bartering—paying for goods with other goods, not money

causeways—raised roads that are built across water

chinampas—plots of land used by Aztec farmers for growing their crops

codices—Aztec books that were folded accordion-style

empire—a large state made up of many countries, all ruled by a leader called an emperor

loincloths—clothing worn by Aztec men, made from strips of cloth tied around their waists and passed between their legs

mosaics—patterns made of tiny pieces of stone or tile

pochteca—Aztec merchant-spies

status—a person's rank in society

tortillas—a flat, round type of bread made of maize flour

tributes—goods or money paid to the Aztec emperor by the people he had conquered

Further Resources

FURTHER READING

Baquedano, Elizabeth. *Aztec, Inca, and Maya.* New York: DK Publishing, 2005.

Macdonald, Fiona. *How Would You Survive as an Aztec?* New York: Franklin Watts, 1995.

Steele, Philip. *The Aztec News.* Milwaukee, Wis.: Gareth Stevens, 2001.

ON THE WEB

For more information on this topic, use FactHound.

1. Go to *www.facthound.com*
2. Type in this book ID: 0756519500
3. Click on the *Fetch It* button.

FactHound will find the best Web sites for you.

LOOK FOR MORE BOOKS IN THIS SERIES

ANCIENT CHINESE
ISBN 0-7565-1647-1

ANCIENT EGYPTIANS
ISBN 0-7565-1645-5

ANCIENT GREEKS
ISBN 0-7565-1646-3

ANCIENT MAYA
ISBN 0-7565-1677-3

ANCIENT ROMANS
ISBN 0-7565-1644-7

THE INCAS
ISBN 0-7565-1951-9

THE VIKINGS
ISBN 0-7565-1678-1

Index